Understanding Penny Stock for Beginners

You can Win Big with Penny Stocks

By

Yolanda Washington-Cowan

Understanding Penny Stock for Beginners
You can Win Big with Penny Stocks
Copyright @ 2021

by Yolanda Washington-Cowan
All rights reserved
Published by
B-Inspired Publishing
7285 Winchester Road, Suite 109
Memphis, TN 38125
www.B-Inspiredpub.com
Printed in the United States
First Edition: March 2021

Table of Contents

Introduction

Being financially free is everybody's dream, and you begin to live it the day you stumble upon a factual and systematic way to gain money in the securities market consistently. What you make out of this opportunity to profit consistently is yours to decide. Patience will be required of you but in the end, it will be valuable if you put your head down and work hard towards learning to be successful in trading penny stocks. After all, who hates learning about what is needed to earn more money and be financially free?

There are so many online platforms that will claim they can transform you into an expert in a short while. Here is the truth—you can't be successful in the stock market overnight, and my advice is that you dismiss these thoughts and their messengers. They will paint the picture that you can get started with a hundred dollars while making you believe trading is relatively easy and doesn't require much effort. This is how they toy about with the emotions of people who fall for their lies and should you fall for their lies, you will have none other than yourself to blame.

If you are willing to learn and put in a little more time understanding the Penny Stock market and how it operates, you can learn a trading scheme with strategies ahead of others.

Many markets are wrongly interpreted in the world today and the Penny Stock market is one of them. People with little or no knowledge jump into the market without the skills needed, tools, and other ingredients required to succeed. You know of someone who has made a thousand dollars (whether this is real or someone told you), and humanly, you would want the same for yourself, don't you?

The fact remains that penny stocks have a way of shaming other assets by making a jaw-dropping percentage move, and it doesn't require much money for you to start trading. From my own experience, I can assure you that there is nothing better than making your first productive trade but be aware that penny stocks don't make anyone rich overnight. You must profit consistently. Overnight success is the false belief that is the main reason why many people lose so much money in the penny stock market.

The only way to be consistent with profit-making in penny stocks (or other markets) is to learn how to pull out small size profits in a consistent fashion until you have amassed enough. You can't do this if you don't distance yourself from those who believe in making money overnight.

While the intricacies associated with trading penny stocks could be simplified, the moment you understand how the trade goes, there is no guarantee you will learn them immediately. However, if you dedicate your time to learning and understanding how the market works, you will. Anyone who makes you believe that you will turn your financial status to millions tomorrow if you start trading with a few hundred dollars today is entirely delusional. However, if you believe them, you are delusional too. You need to reexamine your thinking again and again.

These guys parade themselves as experts, and these so-called experts will stop at nothing to convince you to trade penny stocks. However, here's the plan; the only way they can get you to buy penny stocks is to paint an untrue picture about the shares of a particular company they want you to buy. When you invest, they will run

away with your money. Everyone's intention is a headfirst plunge into trading and making money, but here is the truth: if you don't equip yourself with accurate knowledge, you risk being devoured by the stock market. It is suitable to study how trading is done, but the approach you choose to go by is one you must be smart about.

Features of penny stocks:

- The shares traded by a small company are usually at a price below $5per share.
- They can also include the share of individual private companies that do not have an active trading market.
- The trading of the shares is usually done by OTC, such as the OTC bulletin board or OTC link LLC.
- It can also be traded on security exchanges, which could be foreign as well.
- The shares are extremely illiquid, which refers to the stock's state, which cannot be quickly sold for cash without some substantial loss, but you can avoid that when you plan to invest in it in the right way.

Let's get to the basics of penny stock investments, so without any further ado, let's begin!

Chapter 1
Penny stock basics

Warnings related to penny stocks:

The fact is that penny stocks tend to result in a more significant risk than regular stocks. The reason behind this inflated level of risk is not complicated. It has a higher level of risk because of the company that holds these penny stocks. These companies lack:

- Profits
- Minimal operations

In addition to that, these companies are not required to file with the SEC. The trade of these stocks is usually made on pink sheets or OTC bulletin boards.

Due to the lack of buyers as well as sellers, it has low liquidity. This is why the orders are not filled right away, and some even tend to get missed.

Usually, when it comes to buying stocks, the concept that comes to your mind is that the stock market is all about finding a company you believe in and investing in. Now that you have purchased the stock, you hold on to it for years; however, this penny stock market method is different. There is a high chance that your investment

will fall, but you could experience some massive benefits before it fails.

The OTC markets:

The OTC markets do play a huge part when it comes to penny stock investments. The concept of the OTC Bulletin Board was discussed before, but what is that?

The OTC Bulletin Board is an electronic trading service that is operated by the Financial Industry Regulatory authority. This service requires all the companies to meet the minimum standards of keeping up-to-date financial statements. Now the penny stocks that are listed on pink sheets have less information. They may not even fulfill these requirements. This is why you tend to get into a greater risk when it comes to penny stock markets.

Penny stocks can be divided into four tiers.

Four tiers of penny stocks:

Back in the day, the stocks traded under $ 1 were almost always small companies struggling to find their place in the market. The outcome of such securities was that they were unpredictable investments for the investors. Nowadays, the priced securities $1 - $10 still represent unpredictable and risky investments in many cases.

7

These mainly include Biotech, Fintech, and internet sectors. If you are thinking of investing in these securities, you need to be fully prepared for the loss that comes with it. A great understanding of the tier of penny stocks could be beneficial on that matter.

Tier 1 penny stocks:

These are the penny stocks that should be your primary focus. They are listed on the major stock exchanges, which include:

- NASDAQ
- New York Stock Exchange

There is a chance that they can be higher, but they are usually priced below $5 per share. They are held to a higher standard than OTC penny stocks because they have to provide financial information to the exchange. This means that they are also less open to manipulation.

Tier 2 penny stocks:

These are the traditional penny stocks, and they have prices between $1 and 99 cents. They can be commonly seen on NASDAQ and NYSE. They cannot be lesser than 1 cent.

They can be delisted if they don't meet the listing requirements, which are generally above $1. These companies tend to get a letter related to the requirements they need to get fulfilled. They are given a certain amount of time to do that, and when they do it, they get listed.

- **Tier 3 penny stock:**

These are the sub-penny stocks that are traded below one penny per share. These types of companies are hardly ever seen on NASDAQ and NYSE. This is because these companies are not strong enough to have the stocks priced at one penny per share. This means that they would start at .0099, which is not the best option for trading the penny stocks.

- **Tier 4 penny stock:**

These are called the triple zero stocks as they are priced between 0.0001 and 0.0009 cents per share. Many of the "hot penny stock" alerts are on sub-penny stocks or trip zero stocks, and they primarily benefit the ones who buy the stock first.

Why choose penny stocks:

It is often said that you make quick progress in the stock market. For this reason, many individuals are attracted to

the concept of penny stocks. As mentioned before, you tend to lose money when investing in penny stocks, but then why would you choose to invest in the first place?

It often aids that the higher the risk is, the higher the chance of potential returns. When you tend to invest in the right companies, you could get enormous returns. Before investing in penny stocks, you need to accept all the warnings and their risks.

The main reason that why people tend to invest in it despite the associated risk is straightforward. It is mainly because when you choose the right stock, you can double or triple your money in a very short amount of time. If you tend to choose a company that grows year after year, it will make sure that you will hold the stock for as long as you can, and there will be no limit to the amounts of gain that you will make!

Some penny stocks are companies that run a profitable business with the motive of potential for their growth. Although these companies do start as penny stocks, they have the potential to grow into large-cap stocks. This will also lead to a tremendous amount of gain, especially for early investors.

You need to invest in penny stocks with the same mindset of investing in a normal stock. You need to make sure that you do your due diligence before making any investment decisions.

Can I Invest in Penny Stocks?

Investing in penny stocks is not for everyone, especially for those who are not mentally prepared to face loss. You should be more than okay with the thought of losing 50-100 percent of your investment in a short period. But as you know that you can gain many great attributes just by choosing the right company, you should try.

How to invest:

Here are the steps that you need to follow if you want to invest in penny stock markets.

Do complete research:

You need to do your complete due diligence when it comes to investing in penny stocks. This includes:

- Doing a reading through the income and cash flow statements.

- This reading will give you a better understanding of what is profitable and what is not.
- You need to check the balance sheet to compare the company's assets versus its debts.

- You need to watch corporate presentations to better understand the type of brand you are thinking of investing in.

- This will make you choose a legitimate company, and it will eliminate the obvious scams that will come your way.

Choose your broker:

You need to find the best brokers for your penny stock investment. You need to make sure that the brokers you are willing to choose do not indulge in extra surcharges. Some of the examples of companies who don't charge additional surcharges are:

- TD Ameritrade
- Trade Station

These companies also do not even charge extra on large orders. There are a lot of brokers who do tend to charge on extra orders. Some also require you to trade the penny stocks by setting up limits on the trades you can execute.

Determination of which stock to trade:

The next step that you need to do is to determine the stock that you want to trade. If you have just started with this, then the best option for you would be OTC markets

websites. They also tend to organize securities into tiered marketplaces. In this way, you can easily determine which stocks are the best to trade and which are not. You can also predict the success of the company in which you will invest in. Finding the right kind of stock is a game-changer.

Chapter 2
Styles of Trading

The world is progressing with digital technology and other advanced creations in the digital world. So many individuals are taking advantage of this opportunity of advancements in penny stock investment as well. Because of this proliferation in technology and the internet, many investors are now willing to buy and sell stocks for themselves online instead of paying the advisors huge amounts of money to trade for them.

This saves them the commission that they usually need to pay, considering the traditional way. However, there are different types of orders, and this chapter will learn all the basic types of stock and how they can meet up your investing style.

Whatever your investing style is, you can use different stock types to do your trading more effectively. There are two major types of orders that every investor should know about. These include:

- Marketing order
- Limit order

Market Order:

A market order is the most basic type of trade. In this order, the buying and selling are done immediately at what its current price is. If you buy a stock, you will pay a near or the same price as the posted stock asked. If you sell a stock, then the stock price will be received the same as the posted bid.

You need to keep in mind that the price at which the last trading is done is not necessarily the price at which the market's order will be executed. The trade can also deviate from the original marketplace. This usually happens in volatile markets. The market orders guarantee an immediate execution of the order, but the prices are not guaranteed.

This type of order is especially preferable for investors who do not want any delay. The main benefit of this type of order is that you will get the trade executed quickly. The only drawback is that you will not know the exact price of it.

Limit Orders:

A limit order is often also called a pending order. This order enables the investors to buy or sell the securities at a specific price in the future. This order is mostly used to

execute the trade once the price has reached the predefined level. The order won't be filled if it hasn't reached this level. This type of order usually sets up a maximum or a minimum price at which you are willing to buy or sell something.

There are four types of limit orders:

- Buy limit
- Sell limit
- Buy stop
- Sell stop

The cost of market and limit orders:

When the investor decides to choose between the two orders, they must know how much the orders will cost. They should be fully aware of the added cost that comes with the orders. Mostly the cost for the market order is typically lesser than that of a limit order. This difference in the commission could range from just a couple of dollars to up to $10. It could be more than $10 as well.

For example, the commission on a market order of $ 10 could be increased up to $ 15 when there is a limit restriction. The most important concept is that you need

to make sure that it's worthwhile to plan on making a limited order.

This could be explained; let's say the broker you are working with charges you $ 7 for a market order and $ 12 for a limit order. There is a specific stock; let's say that stock is X. So this X stock is trading at $ 50 per share. But the problem is that you want to buy it for $49.09. When you get ten shares in a market order, you pay a total of $ 507, including the commission price in it. On the other hand, by placing a limit order, you will generally pay $ 511.

In the case of a market order, you will lose some money in the added cost of it, and while in the case of the limit order, the stock won't fall less, it will only increase, which can make it difficult for you to buy it.

Some more stock order types:

Here are some additional instructions and restrictions that different brokerages can allow you to get.

Stop Loss order:

This is also known as the stop market. This is said to be the most useful order. It is helpful because it is different than the limit and market orders. This order remains resting until a specific price is passed, whereas the limit

and market orders become active instantly. It is then activated as a market order after some time.

When it gets transformed into a market order, the shares are sold at the best price available to them. This order is best for those who have a hard time keeping up a continuous check with the market. This will also protect them if a sudden downside occurs during that time.

Stop-limit order:

These are kind of similar to the stop-loss orders. The only difference is that they have a limit. The limit is set upon the price at which it will be sold. There two prices at which the stop limit sets itself:

- The stop price, which generally converts the order to a sell order
- Then there is the limit price.

What this type of order does is that it converts the sell order into a limit order, which then only executes at a limit price or even a better price. This is a problem for the stop-loss order as it can get triggered with the flash crash.

All or none:

This type of order is specifically designed for the trading of penny stocks. This is important for the people who will buy the penny stocks because this ensures that as an investor, you get either the whole quantity of the stock that you requested or none at all. This is not suitable if the stock is very illiquid. It can also be problematic if there is a limit set on the stocks.

Immediate or Cancel:

This type of order ensures that if there are no shares traded in that immediate time, the order can be canceled completely. The immediate time interval is very short can be of just a few seconds or even less.

Good Til Cancelled:

This is a time restriction that you can pay on different orders. A good til canceled order will remain active until you decide to cancel it. In this case, the brokerages will limit the maximum time, and you can keep the order open for three months.

Day:

In case you don't set up a specific expiration time in the Good Til Canceled order, then the order will be presented as a day order. This means that the order will

expire after the day ends. If it isn't filled, then you would have to re-enter it the following day.

It is important to know the difference between a market and a limit order. Both can be turn out to be appropriate in use when it comes to the type of investment approach you adopt. If you are a long-term investor, then you should go for the market order. It is also cheaper. If you are a trader who is willing to seek benefits in the charts' short-term trends, you should limit order with the stop-loss order. In this way, you will understand the type of orders and how they can impact your trading. You can choose the one that goes best with your investment.

You need to be aware of all the tips and tricks in penny stocks so that you can avoid scams and make the most out of your investments.

Chapter 3
How to Trade Penny Stocks

Finding a Good Broker

When you want to choose a stockbroker, be sure the broker supports penny stocks since most brokers don't. You might also want to ensure they're willing to trade in other markets than The New York Stock Exchange (NYSE) or the National Association of Securities Dealers Automated Quotations (NASDAQ). Most stockbrokers favor trades done through the markets mentioned above and other prominent ones, but most penny stocks don't trade there; instead, they trade the pink sheet. They are traded only on the OTCBB, which means Over the Counter Bulletin Board. You must be sure your broker supports this before choosing them.

Another marker to watch for is low commissions. While trading on high-priced stocks like $70, $150, or $500 trades, a $5 commission for a broker isn't big at all. But when it comes to Penny Stocks, $5 could buy a hundred shares or more or might represent a considerable part of your profit at the end of the day. Settling for a broker with a lower fee is essential, but its importance to the Penny Stock world can't be overemphasized.

Stockbrokers are very important and play a significant role in the stock market. They furnish investors with the essentials needed for trading and they can influence how the investors trade. When you want to hire a penny stockbroker, one view you must pay attention to is their fee. Most of the stockbrokers demand commissions for every amount you invest. The rates are often fixed for a particular number of stocks, and then when more stocks are added, the fees may differ. It's much better to search for a broker who, regardless of the number of shares bought, puts forward a flat rate for each trade. If the flat rate is low, the impact commissions will have on the profit will be small. Weighing the areas of concern stated above and the risks related to trading penny stocks, penny stockbrokers and their roles generates more interest. It is all-important to pick out the proper advisors for high-risk investments like penny stocks.

Penny Stock Day Trading

One effective way to trade on the penny stock market and make profits is by day trading. It doesn't require many technicalities to start; hence it isn't difficult and with proper knowledge, you may begin to turn in profits in a matter of days. Bear this in mind as we proceed: genuine day traders focus more on options and

derivatives, which are high in volatility and expose the traders to more risks, unlike penny stocks and other conventional equities. Therefore, going by its definition, penny stocks are impossible to be day traded; however, making profits daily is possible on penny stocks because it is a highly volatile market.

Primarily, Day trading requires that you are abreast of many stocks. The majority of these stocks will not make an unusual move daily, so it advisable you have a set of stocks you would want to choose from at any time.

All of the shares on your database or list must be attracting new investors and with a high trading interest (should be trading more than 50,000 shares per day) and must be volatile. Beware, most penny stocks might experience many activities due to their daily volatility but can become a desert overnight. Spend time looking at the trading volumes across a more extended chart to ensure the shares on your list are desirable.

What Is Day Trading?

Day trading simply means taking advantage of the fluctuations that occur in the stock market. For instance, you can purchase an issue at $0.10 and sell the following week or the next hour for $0.20, affording you a few

percentage points on whatever you invested. If you spot a more significant profit than 25%, you shouldn't hesitate to take it. Repeat this a few more times and huge returns will be left staring at you, which could be seen as a profitable investment strategy.

There is always a downside to every investment and day trading isn't an exception. If you purchase an issue and its value drops, you will be left with two options; either stop the loss by canceling the trade or wait until another opportunity presents itself, meaning your money is stuck till that time. However, what If that time never comes and you end up losing your entire investment? This may not be an issue for traders who do have enough assets with them because while one stock falls in value with a fragment of their money tied up, the other set remains active and can be used.

If you must leverage day trading and avoid risking all your money yet profit maximally, then you must read the next paragraph over and over again and align your style of investment to it.

Objectives of Penny Stocks Day Trading

If you must be successful in Penny Stock Day Trading, you must pay attention to what I am about to tell you.

Everybody's general aim is to turn in hundreds of percentages on investments, year in and year out. However, this isn't meant to be achieved in a minute but slowly accumulates a few percentages over time. This is where most of the trading strategies collapse – most traders do not know that walking away with smaller profits is better than waiting for a longer time to make profits.

These are the goals you must set for effective trading and they are as follows:

• Small earnings of 10-25% would appear frequently. Don't wait till the profits are higher; take them as they present themselves.

• Place your orders with the stocks' actions where you can see them so that you won't be caught off guard when there is a change.

The good part is that in day trading, company fundamentals and the market's general activities are less significant. Your focus is mainly on stocks' day-to-day fluctuations instead of what the market looks like or what the companies earn. Buying a stock when the price

falls and selling it when it increases equals success and this is independent of trends or the "face of the Market."

What matters the most is that your eyes are fixed on the market and the trading activities within it rather than on the companies you invested in - whether they have a good future or not. This is important: identify the trading ranges and either buy or sell as you deem fit.

Day trading is free from ambiguity and is straightforward. Nonetheless, to be successful you will need to combine patience, luck, and knowing when to collect your profit as soon as it shows up. With your eyes on the stock market and a clear strategy, day trading becomes easy, requiring fewer thoughts but yielding huge stock returns.

Brokerage firm

A brokerage firm also called a brokerage company, acts as a conversational partner, connecting traders synchronically with the buyers to initiate a transaction. These companies receive a token in commissions (which are either a percentage of a certain amount a trader used during a transaction) as soon the transactions are completed. For instance, if a trader places an order for a stock of his choice and is executed, a transaction fee is

paid by the trader for the efforts the brokerage firm put in to complete the transaction.

The Purpose of a Brokerage Company

If everyone had full knowledge of what they were meant to do and act on it quickly and with accuracy, there wouldn't be a need for brokerage companies. Buyers may not always know who the sellers are and at what prices they are offering them, likewise sellers. This is why brokerage firms exist; to provide assistance to their clients by bringing both buyers and sellers together to agree at a specific price while collecting a commission for rendering those services.

There are various kinds of brokerage companies that offer multiple types of services that flood the financial market. We will discuss the three primary forms of brokerages briefly.

Full-service brokerage services: this kind of brokerage company works with financial experts whose duty is to provide advice and support and help handle or negotiate investments. Brokerages that deliver such services are usually expensive.

Discount Brokerage Services: These brokerages typically charge less than traditional brokers, although they can't provide their clients with a personal

27

relationship found in the full-service brokerages. They allow the investor to do their research through a computerized system for a lower commission. With the recent push for zero commission on online trades, the Robo-advisors were introduced.

Robo-Advisors Services: this is an automated platform that advises clients on investments. They are financial advisors who took investment management digital, carrying out their services using algorithms that don't require any form of human intervention at a very low price. Several of these brokerage firms include no fees or commissions and one could start for as little as $5-10 in most cases.

There are many regulated stockbrokers in the United States of America and here is a list of a few of these brokers. They are not listed in any particular order and this isn't an in-depth list:

- **Choice Trade**: They are registered with the SEC (Securities and Exchange Commission) and offer penny stocks on two markets; the Over the Counter Bulletin Board (OTCBB) and Pink Sheet. Their penny stock brokerage charges range between Commission-free, $5 Stock Plan A and B customers and $7 for other kinds of

stock trades. An extra $0.0007 charge is applied per share for shares above 10,000.

- **Charles Schwab Corp:** With these stockbrokers, penny stocks can be traded through their trading accounts. With their website, you can trade OTCBB and pink sheets online. Their charges are $4.95 for each trade.

- **Interactive Brokers:** They have selected stocks that offer penny stock on the Over the Counter Bulletin Board (OTCBB) and on the pink sheet securities through their trading account. They have a constant-grade structure and a leveled structure. Regular pricing begins from $0.005 for each share in a $100 trade, while the tiered pricing from $0.005 per share for over 100 million volumes each calendar month.

- **Scottrade:** They offer penny stock at the rate of $6.95 per trade and an additional 0.5% on the below $1 per share. Unlike the brokers mentioned earlier, Scottrade provides screening instruments to provide selective data on penny stocks, which will help a trader make the right decisions. These selective data comprise quotes,

news, and commentaries regarding the market and reports.

- **TD Ameritrade:** Like other brokers, they take orders listed on the Over the Counter Bulletin Board as well as the Pink Sheet market. These trades can be carried out on the standard trading accounts provided by them. The charges are the same with Scottrade at $6.95 for each trade. This applies to all penny stocks.

Outside the list mentioned above, you can purchase penny-stock shares via your regular stockbroker. If you choose to explore another brokerage, these are some questions you might want to ask and central points you should consider. To meet up with clients' demands, virtually all brokers provide their clients with trading apps on both phones and PCs. Sole reliance on phone calls and other traditional trade facilities could lead to unwanted results when prices fluctuate while waiting for the one taking an order to pick up the phone and take your orders. This can affect your trade importantly as price fluctuation happens in seconds. Also, you may incur more charges for the call you made. Brokerages that offer Self-help alternatives or a medium to display pricing and relevant information are much better than

waiting for a broker to pick up the phone and take your orders; you would avoid paying extra charges for the phone calls.

Steps to Opening a Brokerage Account

Here are a few steps to take while opening a brokerage account:

- Choose the form of report you need
- Consider the characteristics you want, their prices and bonuses
- Examine the services rendered
- Make up your mind on the Brokerage firm that fits what you want
- Start filling the application for a new account
- Fund your new account and begin investing.
- Begin exploring investments

Chapter 4
Finding the Right Penny Stocks

One of the many sides of the challenge in ascertaining the best possible way to make money while trading penny stocks is discovering the right stock. Finding a depreciated or low stock in value is a big task to start with because nearly all investors have stocks that they feel will yield plenty of returns on their watch list. While trading penny stocks, finding a depreciated stock with good value, stable, and promising prospects is what you need.

Since no one goes into trading penny stocks planning to lose, you will have to be on the lookout for someone willing to sell at a reasonable price. Most traders refuse to sell if they perceive the company is expected to make a turnaround. They would prefer holding on so they can reap whatever rewards that will come as a result. However, this will, in turn be difficult for you to buy; therefore, you will always find someone willing to sell their stocks for a fair or higher price.

As soon as you have purchased the penny stock you believe has the potential to rise tomorrow, you need to be sure that the right time will come, and you will

eventually sell your stocks. Like most traders, you can keep your shares hoping it will be on-demand shortly, although you bought it for a bargain when it wasn't on-demand. If you try to sell it now, no one will want to buy it because it isn't on-demand yet.

Having put all these concepts into consideration, the best possible way of making profits in trading Penny Stocks is finding the right stocks with good value, purchasing them at a low price, and keeping them. Until the company is done restructuring or turning around so you can get back into the market and sell again.

Understanding the market place:

When you are looking to capture profits in the market, you need to do good observation. As you know, penny stocks tend to trade in OTC and pink sheets; their regulation is much less widespread than those in popular exchanges. The major difference between an OTC and a major exchange is how the stocks are evaluated for their quality.

As an investor, you need to keep in mind that companies' opportunity to offer fraudulent shares is possible. This is why you need to do the company's right research that you are willing to choose to invest in. Although SEC has set up certain requirements on the OTC marketplace because there is a chance for a lower bar to entry for companies seeking to sell shares, it has made fraudulent activity.

Researching the right penny stock:

One of the key factors in researching the right penny stock is the history of the company. There are other factors too that could lead to an investment in the wrong type of penny stock. As an investor, you need to avoid small companies that are at risk. Here are the few items

that you need to keep into consideration so that you can identify the wrong penny stock:

Poor Financial State:

It is more than expected in penny stocks for a company to be financially broken. These kinds of companies are under a lot of debt. There are so many debts due to which these companies cannot even pay their interest rates properly. When a company becomes financially broken, there is a high chance that it will go bankrupt and even close down its operations.

Lack of documentation:

This is one of the easiest red flags that you can find in a company. If the company does not have enough documentation, then it is true that you might end up investing in the wrong type of stock. There is some extra information provided, which is outside the online homepage of the company. If you do not find any extra information, you can undergo fraudulent activity.

The best way to do your research is by doing it online. Consider all the factors mentioned above when you are doing your research on the stock's right company.

Evaluating the penny stock shares:

After doing heavy research, you need to select multiple small groups to make potential investments. Once you have selected that, then it is time to do a critical evaluation of the details of the shares as well.

You need to be able to identify the following details:

- The total number of shares
- The number of outstanding shares
- Planned activities that will help you share price by diluting
- The frequency of the issuance of the new shares
- Any stock options that are offered

The share price should not be the only factor that should be kept in consideration. Its price may not always determine the quality of a firm. This is why it is always important to consider the number of shares that are available. It is considered a general rule that the more shares that find their way into a marketplace, the harder it becomes for the outstanding shares to gain their values. Let's say that a company is seeking funding; the new shares' issuance will dilute the current pricing and reduce the value of all the existing shares.

Beware of dilution:

Dilution is another factor that needs to be considered when it comes to investing in penny stocks. The number of shares that are outstanding can become out of control due to the use of employee stock options. If a company issues share for the motive of raising the capital, then it can dilute the ownership percentage, which is held by other investors.

For example, let's say a company named X. Company X issued an extra 100 million just to raise the capital; then, the share price would decrease to $0.09. This means that the number of shares has changed and not the business itself as a whole.

When you are looking to invest in penny stocks, you need to be vigilant about the company with a strong force on its shares. If there is a dilution constantly, then there is a high chance that the existing shares' value will wear down.

You need to be aware of these concepts when you are looking to invest in penny stocks.

Using a stock screener to find penny stocks:

As you know, selecting a good stock is not easy as there is a chance of fraudulent activities and companies that are not stable. Finding the accurate right stock that meets up your parameters can be possible through stock screeners. A stock screener is a great way to find the exact type of penny stock you are looking for. They are invaluable, and any investor could get them and use them for their benefit.

What are the stock screeners?

Stock screeners are defined as automated tools that find the stocks that meet the criteria you set. This is a great and inexpensive way to find the right types of penny stocks that meet your criteria. They can clarify the thousands of potential penny stock investments down to hundreds, or it can even do it up to a few dozen or the criteria you set up for it to find.

How it works:

The best notion about stock screeners is that it's a digital work. The screen does all the work for you. The outcome of the search that you do is accurate, and it is hardly ever wrong.

For example, let's say that you set up a parameter of shares between one to two dollars; now, the screen will eliminate all the other stocks that do not meet your criteria and only give you the stocks that meet your requirements. It has three components, which are:

- A database of companies
- A set of variables
- A screening engine whose job is to find the companies and satisfy those variables and generate a list of matches for you

Where to find it?

You can find stock screeners through many great websites that are financial, for example - Google Finance!

Many stockbrokers also provide them. There are also different types of screen stockers that you can find. You can add stock screeners with advanced features by just paying a small fee. In this way, you can also access screening that is done by technical analysis.

Limitations:

There are certain limitations attached to the stock screeners as well. This means that you can only assess and sort the available data about the shares of the

company. This includes the price, market, and industry group. As a screener, you cannot eliminate or sort shares based on anything other than the data that is related to the stock itself. These criteria are out of the reach of the screener:

-        Underlying operations of the company
-        Underlying companies
-        Prospects of the company

Be on the lookout for penny stocks with increasing volume:

You need to watch some of the stocks that have been with increasing volumes. This is the most common factor that develops interests in these stocks. However, if you choose some stocks that are growing more than the normal volumes of stocks, you need to be aware that something isn't right.

Some of the penny stocks that you need to look out for, for now, are the following, but you needed to keep up with the latest trends of then penny stock markets:

-        Trevena, Inc.
-        Aqua bounty Technologies Inc.
-        New Gold, Inc.
-        Aytu Bioscience, Inc.

These are just some suggestions relating to the prevailing situation; you are free to choose whatever kind you want depending on your criteria and preference.

Chapter 5
How to Identify Winning Penny Stocks

Be on the lookout for profitable and cheap stocks

Whenever you spot a company that has been identified as a winner and notice their stocks are tendered at a relatively inexpensive rate, it may be a scam popularly known as a pump and dump. Pump and dump is a scam stock where the promoters sell the shares to unsuspecting victims and finally crash the stocks to make gains. Investing in this kind of stock won't deliver any returns. So the best and only way to verify that a stock is good and worthwhile before you invest is, firstly, do thorough research on the company. Secondly, companies that are sprouting or making their way back from bankruptcy and are undergoing restructuring are highlighted for suitable investments. Their shares will be sold at a relatively low price as they are either new or undergoing restructuring. The more successful they become, the more their stocks will rise.

Monitor the price of your stock

Traders who want to be successful should be able to spend every day sitting before their Personal Computers, pulling off trades and making profits as well. This is

how successful traders do it; this is how they stay up all day just to win trades. While this kind of trading appears to many traders as running a risk, a bit of luck can be helpful. Unlike a gambling casino, however, traders don't have any idea of the ratio of winning before they put in their wealth; naturally, no one has a way of predicting luck.

This is how to overcome this: by spending ample time reexamining, exploring and researching, and monitoring your stock, in no time you will begin to notice some patterns that will help you determine when to buy or sell a stock.

Chapter 6
Risks and rewards of penny stocks

Rewards of Trading Penny Stocks

Like every other investment form, some advantages and disadvantages come with investing or buying company shares or stocks. Hence, it is paramount you have enough knowledge before the investment you want to make (no matter the company), whether they are small businesses or multinationals. Below are the major merits of Penny Stock:

• The main reward of Penny Stock remains that it doesn't require a huge sum of money to start. They are investments below $5 and the prices of their shares are low and cheap.

• It is easier to purchase penny stocks since they are common and can be accessed by anyone, anytime. Since penny stocks don't come at a high price, it enables traders or investors to acquire more stock. This provides traders with multiple options of investing their monies in different penny stocks simultaneously and at a relatively low price, without worries. On a larger scale, it makes it easier for investors who trade wisely and monitor stock

fluctuations to generate more profits in their investments.

• Why most people opt for penny stocks is because of their volatility. This creates a chance for them to rake in some money within a short interval. For instance, if you buy shares worth $1000 and overnight the stocks you purchased double, that just doubled your money.

• Often, some shares could rise and their values triple. After the shares have increased, they are traded as shares with market capitalizations (Mid-Cap). To be successful in penny shares, you need to have developed some skills, like patience, gathering information from a reliable broker who is skilled in investments without losing much money, investing little money at a time, and being alert and smart. The reason for trading is to profit at the end of the day, but now, you are armed with the right knowledge. Don't forget; it is a risky business.

Risks of Trading Penny Stocks

• Penny stocks got their popularity from their unparalleled advantages, but that doesn't eliminate the disadvantages it has as well. While the potential of making a huge amount of profit is there, the probability of you losing all your monies is high as well. I believe

people lose more than they gain because they fail to understand how the market operates and what thrives there. Buying these shares looks easy, but the problem is getting someone to buy from you. So, the stocks' illiquidity is one of its major challenges, which is why it is a very risky business.

• Often, new investors may find it hard to detect when a company that is running bankrupt issues out some stocks, investing in such stock will increase the chances of them losing their money. More so, when new companies bring out penny stocks and the prices don't rise, you stand the chance of losing your investments. A lack of adequate information is the major reason unsuspecting investors invest in new or bankrupt companies.

• The advent of scammers has ensured that investors are lured into investing in stocks that are hyped so that demand and prices of these stocks increase. Once the scammers have noticed the prices are inflated, they will crash the stocks and make away with investors' money. The only people who will benefit from the promoters and showmen bought before the scammers took over and sold some shares to investors when the prices were high.

This leaves the new investors with shares that have no value anymore.

• People who claim to know their way around the penny stock market get scammed or could encounter trouble, which is common to penny stocks, because most of the companies don't have a financial or management record and could be on the verge of running aground without the investor knowing.

• Penny Stocks are normally traded by new investors or greenhorns who are getting acquainted with the market as most experts don't trade penny stocks because of their volatility. The truth is, these stocks won't keep rising all the time, and there is a time when the value drops and the prices remain the same or drops and this discourages people from buying.

• Penny stocks are predictable. People could predict the movement of most penny stocks' prices, especially when there's information that a company is about to take a substantial leap or is hitting a breakthrough. However, in a case where the company you bought shares from isn't making significant progress per the time your shares lie dormant, and investors lookout for where they will gain the most.

• Penny stocks have a high illiquidity rate. If you are stuck and need some money, the tendency that you will find a buyer is low and you might be forced to wait until the companies you invested in making a significant financial move, which will, in turn, attract investors to sell. Under normal circumstances, it is difficult to sell off penny stocks because traders don't buy much every day in the stock market. Like we established earlier, the prices and values of shares can nosedive in minutes. As a new and inexperienced investor, it would be wise not to have only penny stocks on your watch list or sets of investments.

While there are risks and moments of doubts here and there when trading Penny Stocks, it remains a good choice for anyone who chooses to trade it. Nonetheless, all that you need is a willingness to take risks and quick thinking, and then you will realize trading Penny Stocks can be worth it and can be a good source of making money.

Despite all the risks mentioned above and pullbacks associated with trading Penny Stocks, the majority of the traders choose to capitalize on this pitfall to make a profit. Penny Stocks are beginner investors who first

start trading and will remain popular amongst them for these reasons: They are inexpensive investments for those who don't want to take big risks and can offer a considerable profitable return. Now that you have acquired enough knowledge about Penny Stocks, you will hopefully win big with penny stocks.

Chapter 7
Are Penny Stocks Illegal?

There is nothing illegal about penny stocks, although scammers frequently use them in various ways to perpetrate financial scams across the globe. Like in the Pump and Dump strategy, a handful of investors or traders come together to balloon the prices of a specific stock for the sole purpose of selling to unsuspecting investors and walking away. The stock eventually crashes and the victims are left in the hot seat, bitter and insincere regret. Other groups of companies that deal with penny stocks don't have a track record of themselves, making false predictions and fraud easy.

You should never forget penny stocks that let you invest in companies that can't boast of a credible financial record. Intrinsically, the last time you might see your money again might be the minute before you invested it. Companies that deal with Penny Stocks are never found on the major stock markets, may not yield as much profit as those on the major markets, and are restrained in operations, as well as resources. You can never predict any of these companies' success if you don't have information, to a feasible extent, about them.

Companies whose assets are above $10 Million and have 500 or more shareholders are usually regulated by the Security and Exchange Commission (SEC), which is why most penny-stock companies are not mandated to register financial statements. The result is, potential investors are at their own risk if they choose to invest. Meanwhile, The SEC regards penny stocks as high-risk investments and expects potential investors to be aware of the risks before they step in.

Therefore, investors should ready themselves for eventualities prevalent in penny stocks because there is a possibility of losing their investments or more while trading penny stocks.

Penny stocks aren't bad, but people need to realize that the penny stock market is not as friendly as it seems. It is one stock traded publicly by companies in the Fiscal Market, of which most of them aren't real companies and why scammers use them to trap customers. The truth is that there are a majority of these companies whose addresses never exist or are in a forgotten garage and have just one employee or can be traced to the backyard of a low-income family. Hence, investors need to be alert to avoid running the risk of losing their monies.

Subsequently, the rules regulating the Penny Stock Market are considerably low, so these companies have no business with reporting a truckload of financial data with the regulating agencies like the Securities and Stock Exchange Commission (SEC) and Financial Industry Regulatory Authority (FINRA). This attracts many of these individuals, who practice corruption to trade penny stock to benefit from new investors who haven't understood the market's language.

Be on the lookout for scammers in penny stocks that function in a central area within the stock market. While Penny Stock isn't the only corrupt market (as some parts of Wall Street are also), it functions in another world or realm well outside reality. Every month, vast sums of money are moved into unclear penny stocks that are just registered corporations. They don't have a net income; no revenue and balance sheets are always empty and without cash. They have no products and services associated with their company, but they work hard to make people believe they do. These companies rank among the worst companies in the world.

Nonetheless, they see the prices of their shares rise as high as 100% in a matter of time. Fortuitously, investors

or traders who are well informed could profit from this information and exploit the opportunities presented by these companies. When you have finally unraveled what once was a mystery about the penny stock market and what goes on in the rear, fear disappears and you will no longer be afraid of penny stocks. Instead, you will welcome them primarily for the enormous opportunities it brings to the fore.

Chapter 8
Don't Be Misled, Avoid Promotions, Bribes, and Scams

Many fraudulent promoters in the penny stock market are in search of gaining benefits from innocent investors. The scams in penny stocks investing are one of the greatest risks this stock has.

Stock Scams:

Stock scams are a phenomenon that is considered to be a very deceptive activity. In this, some stock markets tend to induce investors to decide on purchasing and selling. This purchasing and selling are done based on the information, which is not true. This results in losses, and this type of activity also violates the security laws.

Lift and Crash Strategies:

This is the most common strategy adopted by the scammers, and many people have been a victim of this type of scam. It is a scheme that attempts to lift the stock price and that too, with false recommendations or misleading statements. The most preferred medium that is adopted by these types of scammers is social media.

They even tend to do this with the help of certain apps, which include Discord or Telegram. The promoters of

this kind of scam then tend to spread rumors, misinformation, and hype. What this does is that it artificially increases the interest in the security. They also drive their prices up. Once the stock price increases to a sufficient amount with almost unsusceptible marks, the promoters tend to sell their stocks at very high prices.

Reverse Merger:

As the name suggests, a privately owned company tends to merge with a public company in this type of stock. In this way it the penny stocks tend to get publicly sold. They publicly trade the stocks without engaging in the traditional way of being enlisted and meeting the SEC's standards to publicly do the trading. This saves the promoters from the expenses and the hassle that comes with the penny stocks' public trading. This type of scams makes it easier for private companies to make the wrong information related to earnings. This also falsely inflates the stocks. Some reverse mergers can also be legitimate; however, most of them are not usually legitimate.

The Experts Scam:

Anyone who has an advertising budget can turn out to be a guru. Unfortunately, they tend to gain a lot of following due to this reason. In this type of false

advertising, the promoter tends to promise to reveal a secret that the financial expert used to acquire a car or an expensive house. The expert tends to promise to reveal all the secrets of the penny stock trading with you for a one-time low sum.

Avoiding scammers:

Now that you know these scammers, here are some suggestions that can eventually make you avoid these scammers.

Promotion and research:

The promoters often hire writers to write false reports about themselves, which are extremely flattering to look at. The issue is that these false reports look familiar to legitimate reports. The key here is to know the difference between stock promotion as well as equity research. Another way to find out is by reading the ending of the report carefully.

Grade the quality:

You need to grade the quality of the management. Its management determines a company's success, and the same goes for the penny stocks one. For this reason, you need to check out the records of the company and judge them based on their success and failures.

Evaluating the financials:

See the balance sheet of the company to figure out if the company has any substantial debts. You should also see the amounts of net cash that are on hand. The key here is to look for the huge growth rate revenues, which will tell you that it's a scam.

Know the quality:

If there is more disclosure provided by the company, the greater will it be its corporate transparency? It is better to know more about the disclosure that the company provides you with.

Chapter 9
You can Win Big with Penny Stocks

Penny stocks are considered a great form of investment for inexperienced people or are on a budget. However, a penny stock is subjected to these two categories of investors; anyone can engage in the penny stock market and start with investing. Some stocks are sold at less than $ 5 per share. You can get multiple shares of these stocks and that too at a significantly lower price than the mainstream market's usual stocks.

Penny stock has two sides to it, and both of these sides are opposite from each other. If it has rewards, then it also has risks attached to it. The key here is to balance both aspects by becoming more aware of the penny stocks' system. This guide will surely make you aware of all the necessary information you need to plan on trading penny stocks.

Trading penny stocks is a great option that should be availed by individuals. You need to find the right penny stocks for it and as well as the right brokers. In this way, you can get valuable profits from investing in penny stocks. There are different styles of trading. You need to adopt the one that is suitable for your investment style.

The most important way to do this is to be aware of all the scams associated with penny stocks.

There is no end to how much profit trading penny stocks can fetch you. Follow the rules, trade, and win big.